FANTÁSTIC FOODS

FRUITS AND VEGETABLES

WRITTEN BY
E.C. ANDREWS

PowerKiDS press

Published in 2025
by The Rosen Publishing Group, Inc.
2544 Clinton Street, Buffalo, NY 14224

© 2024 BookLife Publishing Ltd.

Written by: E.C. Andrews
Edited by: Elise Carraway
Designed by: Jasmine Pointer

Cataloging-in-Publication Data

Names: Andrews, E.C.

Title: Fruits and vegetables / E.C. Andrews.

Description: Buffalo, NY : PowerKids Press, 2025. | Series: Fantastic foods | Includes glossary and index.

Identifiers: ISBN 9781499449044 (pbk.) | ISBN 9781499449051 (library bound) | ISBN 9781499449068 (ebook)

Subjects: LCSH: Fruit--Juvenile literature. | Vegetables--Juvenile literature.

Classification: LCC TX397.A537 2025 | DDC 641.3'4--dc23

Manufactured in the United States of America

CPSIA Compliance Information: Batch #CW25PK. For further information contact Rosen Publishing at 1-800-237-9932.

Find us on 

Image Credits

All images are courtesy of Shutterstock.com. With thanks to Getty Images, Thinkstock Photo and iStockphoto.
Cover – miss.lemon, grey_and, vungnn, BUTENKOV ALEKSEI, Natthapol Siridech, JIANG HONGYAN, New Africa, Brent Hofacke, leonori. 4–5 – ShineTerra, Valentyn Volkov. 6–7 – MAOIKO, Tim UR. 8–9 – Viktor Sergeevich, zoryanchik, NataliaZa. 10–11 – Pixpan_creative, Tatjana Baibakova. 12–13 – Makistock, PixaHub. 14–15 – Krakenimages.com, Nitr. 16–17 – Robyn Mackenzie, Joshua Resnick. 18–19 – PeakStock, udra11. 20–21 – Brent Hofacker, Volodymyr TVERDOKHLIB, Pixel-Shot. 22–23 – MarkoBr, New Africa.

CONTENTS

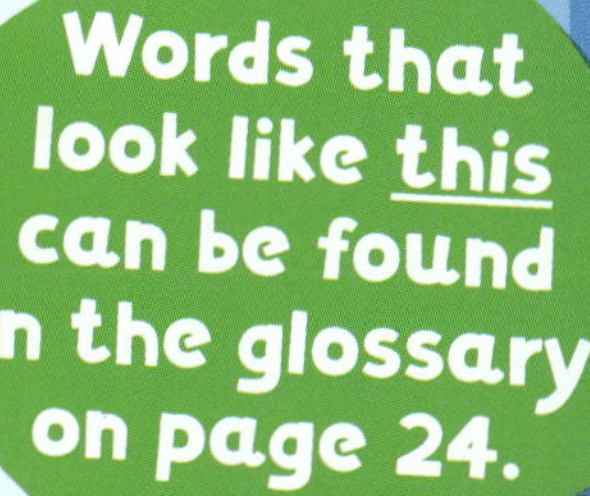

Words that look like this can be found in the glossary on page 24.

DAILY DIET

Do you need to be reminded to eat your vegetables? You might wonder, why does it matter what you eat? If you have eaten enough and you feel full, that should be fine, right?

Well, eating different foods is important for feeling happy and healthy. This is called having a balanced diet. Fruits and vegetables are part of a balanced diet. Let's talk about why!

WHAT Is a FRUIT?

A fruit is a part of a plant that has seeds inside it. Fruits are often sweet and juicy. They can usually be eaten raw. However, not all fruits can be eaten.

Only plants that have flowers grow fruits. Fruits grow after the flowers are <u>pollinated</u>. Anything that has seeds inside it is a fruit. That includes peppers, cucumbers, and tomatoes.

WHAT Is a VEGETABLE?

A vegetable is an <u>edible</u> part of a plant that does not have seeds in it. Some vegetables come from roots, such as beets, carrots, and potatoes. These are called root vegetables.

Other vegetables come from plant stems, such as asparagus and long-stem broccoli. These are called stem vegetables.

Some leaves also count as vegetables. Things such as spinach and lettuce are leafy green vegetables.

FABULOUS FIBER

Fiber is found in <u>plant-based</u> foods. Eating enough fiber is important when it comes to having a balanced diet. It can help you feel full for longer and give you plenty of <u>energy</u> throughout the day.

Fiber is great for your stomach. Having enough fiber in your diet can help you <u>digest</u> your food more easily. Eating fiber can also help keep your heart healthy.

Goodbye BLOATING

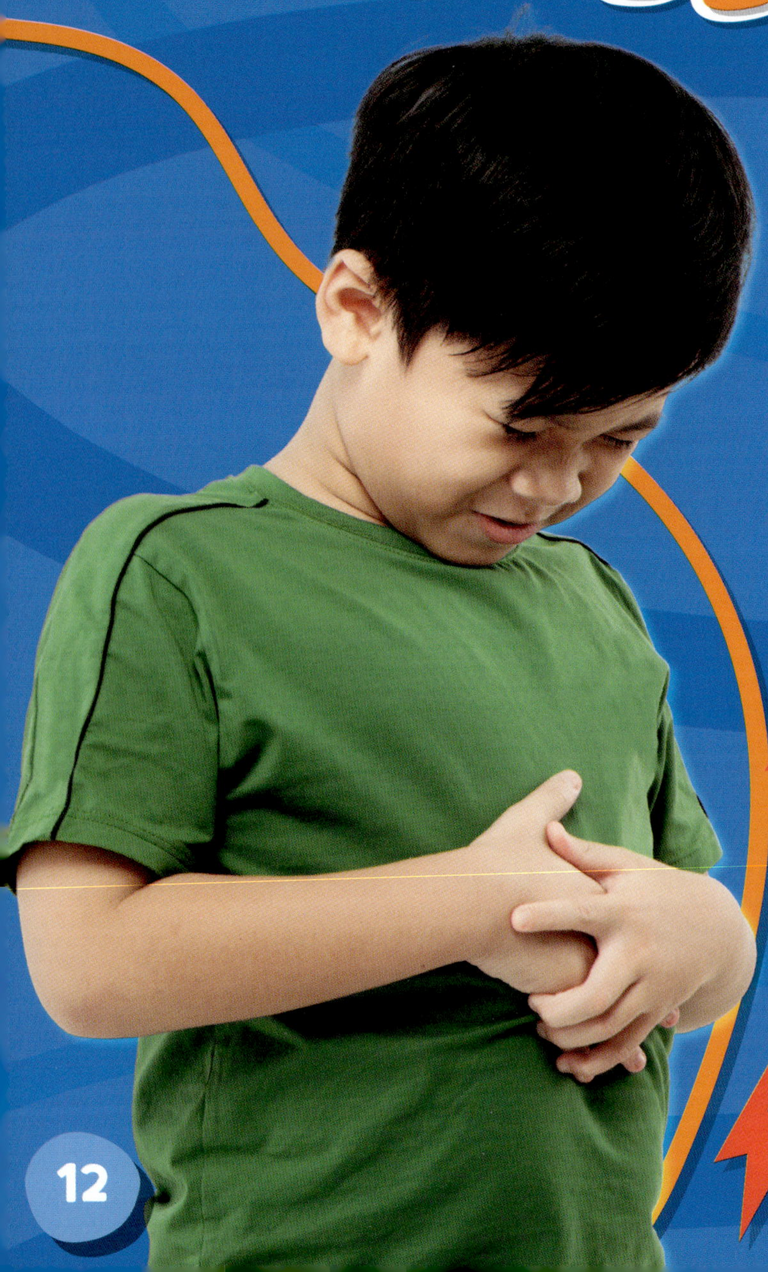

Has your tummy ever felt too tight? Maybe you have had stomachaches too. This could mean that you are bloated. Bloating can be caused by many things. Eating certain fruits and vegetables can help.

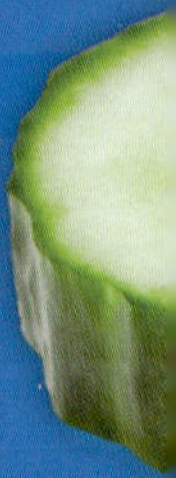

Many fruits and vegetables are high in fiber and water, such as cucumbers and celery. In the right amounts, fiber can help with smooth digestion. Water helps you stay <u>hydrated</u>, so you are less likely to bloat.

HAPPY HEART

Keeping your heart healthy is important. Your heart works hard to keep your body working. Having enough different fruits and vegetables in your diet can help. Yummy fruits such as apples, pears, and oranges are great choices!

As for vegetables, broccoli, leafy greens, and green beans can help keep your heart going strong. If you want to add some color to the plate, try jazzing it up with some tasty carrots.

FEELING FRESH

Did you know that eating enough fruits and vegetables is good for your brain? A healthy brain and body will help bring you enough energy to keep you feeling fresh throughout the day!

Leafy greens can help keep your brain healthy. Root vegetables, such as beets and carrots, have vitamins and minerals that are good for keeping your brain working well. Different berries might help keep your memory strong.

Proper PORTIONS

So, we know that fruits and vegetables are good for us. They can be eaten on their own or with other foods. But how many fruits and vegetables do we need to keep our diet balanced?

A lot of food experts say that eating around five different <u>portions</u> of fruits and vegetables each day is a healthy and balanced amount. This is just a <u>guide</u>, so it is OK if you sometimes eat more or less.

FUN FOOD

Fruits and vegetables can be eaten in lots of different ways. Vegetables can be made into delicious sauces or into kebabs. Leafy greens can give your favorite sandwiches some extra crunch.

Blending your favorite fruits together is an easy way to make a yummy, fiber-filled smoothie — perfect for a hot day. Fruit salads also make delicious desserts. You can use any fruit you want!

21

PERFECT PLATE

Eating fruits and vegetables is fantastic! But remember, they are only one part of your diet. There are lots of other fantastic foods that are needed to keep your diet balanced.

Here are some of the different kinds of foods that should be eaten alongside fruits and vegetables as part of a balanced diet:

GLOSSARY

digest	to break down food into things that can be absorbed and used by the body
edible	safe to be eaten
energy	the power that makes living things able to move and live
guide	a suggested way of doing things
hydrated	to have drunk enough water for the body to work
plant-based	to do with foods made with or out of plants
pollinated	when pollen is passed on from a plant to a plant of the same kind, so that seeds are produced
portions	amounts of a particular food for someone to eat

INDEX